Bible Nurture and Reader Series

From a child thou hast known
The HOLY SCRIPTURES
which are able to make
thee wise unto salvation.

Bible Nurture and Reader Series

We Learn
About God's People

Grade 1
Units 4, 5

Rod and Staff Publishers, Inc.
Crockett, Kentucky 41413
Telephone (606) 522-4348

BIBLE NURTURE AND READER SERIES

"If you train your children carefully until they are seven years old, they are already three-quarters educated." This quote recognizes the importance of the critical early years in molding a child's life. The influences of childhood become powerful, lasting impressions.

The type of schoolbooks used certainly affects the developing appetites of our children for reading material. We will not instill in them appreciation for godly values by feeding them frivolous nonsense. We hold the Bible to be the highest guide for life and the best source of training for our children. The Bible reveals God and His will. Proverbs 9:10 says, "The fear of the Lord is the beginning of wisdom: and the knowledge of the holy is understanding." It is important that our children are exposed to truth from the beginning of their learning experience.

For the student to be exposed to the truth of God's Word only in textbooks is not sufficient to give him the very best. It is necessary for the tutor, be he parent or other teacher, to be firmly rooted in the Word of God and have the power of God's presence in his life. The Bible must be treasured as God's message to mankind. On that conviction this series is built, with the Scriptures as its very substance.

This book is designed as part of a series and will be most useful if so used. The grade one material includes the following books.

Pupil's Reader Unit 1
Pupil's Reader Units 2, 3
Pupil's Reader Units 4, 5

Worksheets Unit 1
Worksheets Units 2–4
Worksheets Unit 5

Phonics Workbook Unit 1
Phonics Workbook Units 2, 3
Phonics Workbook Units 4, 5

Printing Practice Unit 1
Printing Practice Units 2, 3
Printing Practice Units 4, 5

Reading Workbook Unit 1
Reading Workbook Units 2, 3
Reading Workbook Units 4, 5

Teacher's Manual Unit 1
Teacher's Manual Units 2, 3
Teacher's Manual Units 4, 5

Copyright, 1986

First edition, copyright 1964; revisions 1970, 1985

By
Rod and Staff Publishers, Inc.
Crockett, Kentucky 41413

Printed in U.S.A.

ISBN 978-07399-0352-0

Catalog no. 11104.3

16   17   18   19   —   20   19   18   17   16   15   14

Table of Contents

Unit 4

Unit 5

Abraham, Isaac, and Jacob

Unit Four

Memory Verses

Lesson 1

Blessed are the peacemakers. Matthew 5:9

Lesson 6

I will be with him in trouble. Psalm 91:15

Lesson 11

My help cometh from the Lord. Psalm 121:2

Lesson 16

Children, obey your parents in all things. Colossians 3:20

Lesson 21

Be sure your sin will find you out. Numbers 32:23

Lesson 26

Be ye kind one to another. Ephesians 4:32

Why Abram Left Home

Near the place where the tower had been started lived a man called Abram. He had two brothers, but one of these brothers died. The brother who died had a son called Lot.

Abram and his wife and Lot started out with Abram's father to go to the land of Canaan. But they stopped before they got there. Not all of them got into the land of Canaan.

The Lord came and talked to Abram. He told him to leave the land where his family lived. He told him to go to a land that He would show him.

This might have seemed hard for Abram. He had to go away from his father's home if he wanted to obey God. Maybe he did not understand why God wanted him to go to a different part of the earth. He did not know how long it would take him to reach the land that God would show him.

God promised to be with him. God promised to help Abram and he obeyed God. He and his wife took Lot with them. They started to go to the land that God had said He would show him.

Key:

brothers — brother

may + *be* = maybe

promise — promised

Sound:

died   got   hard   leave   left   Lot   part

seemed   started

Learn:

Abram   Abram's   before

Canaan   different

Lesson 2

Where Abram Went

God led Abram to the land of
Canaan. Many other people lived in
this land. They were strangers to
Abram. Most of them did not love
the true God.

Even though Abram was a
stranger in this land, he did not
need to be afraid because God was
with him. God came to Abram and
talked to him after he was in the
land of Canaan. He told him that
someday this land would belong to
him and to his children. Abram
did not have any children. Yet he
believed what God told him.

God said that He would take

the land away from the people who were living there. He would give it to Abram's family instead.

There in the plain Abram worshiped God. But he did not stay in the plain. He went to the mountains. There he worshiped God again. When Abram was in the plain, he remembered God. When he was in the mountains, he remembered God, too. Wherever we are, we should remember God.

There came a hard time in the land of Canaan when there was not enough to eat. So Abram did not stay in Canaan. He went to a land that was not far away. After a time, the king in that land sent them away. They went back again to the land of Canaan.

Key:

be + *long* = belong

remember — remembered

Sound:

far   king   later   plain

Learn:

believed   enough   instead   stranger

strangers   wherever   worshiped

A Quarrel

Abram was a very rich man. He had many animals and much money. God was with him and helped him. So, when Abram went back to Canaan, he had many things to take along with him.

He and his wife and Lot went back to the mountains where they had been before. There again Abram prayed to God.

While Abram was in Canaan, he did not live in a house. He lived in tents.

He often moved from one place to another. He could take down his tent and move to a new place and

then put up his tent again.

Lot had many animals, too. And there was not room for Abram and Lot to live near to each other. They needed more room for their animals.

The men who took care of Abram's animals quarreled with the men who took care of Lot's animals. Abram did not like to have them quarrel. He did not want to quarrel with Lot. He decided it would be better for them not to live so near to each other.

Key:

an + *other* = another

Sound:

along   better   Lot's   needed   prayed

room   tent   tents   while

Learn:

decided   money   move   moved   quarrel

quarreled   their   together

Lot Chooses

God had promised to give to Abram the land of Canaan. He could have taken the best land and let Lot have what was left. But Abram did not do that. He let Lot choose which land he wanted.

Lot looked at the land. He decided to take the land that looked the best. It was a plain and had plenty of water and food for the animals.

Abram took the land that Lot did not want. It did not look so good. But Abram would rather take it than quarrel with anyone.

God came to talk to Abram

after Lot went away. He told him to look east and west. Abram was told to look in every direction. God told him that He would give him all the land that he could see.

It does not seem that it was very kind of Lot to take the best land. And it did not pay him to choose it. Some very bad people lived in the city near Lot. Things did not go well for Lot with such bad people near him.

One time some people came to fight with the people who lived in the city near Lot. They took away all their food and other things. They even took many of the people along with them. They took Lot with them, too.

Abram heard about it. He went

and helped Lot get back to his home again.

Key:

any + *one* = anyone

right — fight

take — taken

Sound:

choose chooses look looked pay

plenty seem such than well

Learn:

city rather

God's Promise to Abraham

When Abram was nearly one hundred years old, God gave him a new name. God came and talked to him. He said, "Your name will not be Abram, but it will be Abraham." This new name meant that he would be a father of many people.

Abraham and his wife had no children. Again God promised Abraham that he would be a father to many people and that He would give him the land of Canaan.

Abraham did not know how it would come to pass, yet he

believed God. He and his wife, Sarah, were old and still did not have any children. But God said that He would give them a son. It was hard for them to believe that they would have a son when they were so old.

Before their little son was born, God told them what to name him. He said they should call his name Isaac. He said Isaac would be born in about one year.

Key:

believed — believe

hundreds — hundred

years — year

Sound:

born   new   pass

Learn:

Abraham   Isaac   meant   nearly   Sarah

Lesson 6

Three Men Visit Abraham

One day Abraham was sitting in his tent door. It was the hot time of the day. When he looked up, he saw three men. Abraham got up and ran to meet them.

He did not know them. They were strangers to him. He was very kind to them. He told them to stay and rest under a tree. He had someone bring water to wash their feet. He gave them good things to eat.

The men asked Abraham, "Where is Sarah, your wife?"

"She is in the tent," said Abraham.

They said, "She will have a son."

Now Sarah was in the tent door behind the man and heard what he said. She laughed when she heard what he said. She did not laugh out loud.

These men who came to visit Abraham were men who were sent from God. They knew that Sarah had laughed. One of the men asked Abraham why Sarah laughed and why she said, "Shall I have a child when I am old?" He asked Abraham, "Is anything too hard for the Lord?" He told Abraham that Sarah would have a son.

Then Sarah was afraid because she had laughed and the men knew it. She said she had not laughed.

But the man said, "No, but you did laugh."

Key:

any + *thing* = anything

some + *one* = someone

Sound:

behind   child   hot   knows   loud   meet

ran   saw   sitting   tree

Learn:

laugh   laughed   shall   visit   wash

Abraham Prays

You remember that in the city where Lot lived, the people were very bad. They were so bad that God was going to destroy them. Abraham was God's friend. God told Abraham what He was going to do. God told Abraham He was going to destroy the city.

Of course, Abraham thought about Lot. Lot was in that city. If God destroyed that city, maybe Lot would be destroyed, too. He did not want Lot to be destroyed.

Abraham asked God, "Will You destroy the godly people with the bad people? If there are fifty godly people in the city, will You destroy the city?"

God said, "If I find fifty godly people in the city, I will not destroy it."

Abraham was afraid there might not be even fifty godly people in the city. So he asked God, "If there are five less than fifty, will You destroy the city?"

"If I find there forty-five, I will not destroy it," said God.

But Abraham was afraid there might not be even forty-five godly people. So he asked, "If there are just forty there, will You destroy it?"

God said, "I will not destroy it."

Abraham was afraid there

would not be even forty godly people in the city. So he asked, "If there are only thirty there, will You destroy it?"

God said, "I will not destroy it."

Abraham asked, "If there are only twenty there, will you destroy it?"

God said, "I will not destroy it."

But Abraham was afraid there might not be even twenty godly people in that large city. So he said, "Oh, Lord, do not be angry, and I will talk just once more. If there are ten there, will You destroy it?"

God said, "If I find ten godly people there, I will not destroy it."

Then the Lord went away, and Abraham went home.

Sound:

fifty   five   forty-five   less   prays

ten   thirty   twenty

Learn:

course   once   thought

Extra Practice:

thought

bought

brought

fought

A Big Fire

The Lord did not even find ten godly people in the large city where Lot lived. But God was kind to Lot because Abraham did not want Lot to be destroyed.

God sent two angels to Lot. They said to him, "Get out of the city. God is going to destroy it." One of the angels told him to take his family along with him.

Lot told his family what God had said. But his sons-in-law did not believe him. They did not believe that God was going to destroy the city. Maybe Lot did not want to go away and leave them. He stayed in the city and tried to get them to come out with him.

The angels wanted Lot to get out of the city even if his sons-in-law would not go along with him. They told Lot to take his wife and two daughters and get out of the city. But Lot did not go. So the angels took them by the hand and brought them out of the city. They told them not to look back.

After they were out of the city, God sent fire from heaven. It burned the city and the people in it. It even burned the good land around the city.

Lot's wife did not obey what God said. She looked back. Because she did not obey, but looked back,

she turned into salt. Now, of all the people who had been in the city, only Lot and his two daughters were safe.

Abraham got up early in the morning. He looked in the direction of the city where Lot had lived. It was going up in smoke. But Lot was not in the city.

Sound:

around   brought   burned   fire

hand   salt   smoke   sons-in-law

stayed   tried   turned

Learn:

angels   daughters   early

Lesson 9

God Helps Hagar

The Lord remembered His
promise to Abraham and Sarah.
And God kept His promise. Yes,
God always keeps His promise.
When Abraham was one hundred
years old, God gave them a son.
They named him Isaac, as God
had told them they should. How
they must have loved him! He was
their only baby. Little Isaac grew
as a baby should.

One day Sarah saw a boy
making fun. This boy's mother
worked for Sarah. Her name was
Hagar. Sarah did not like it that
Hagar's boy made fun. She wanted

Abraham to make her and her son
go away. But Abraham did not
like to do that.

God came to him and told him
that he should do what Sarah said.
Abraham obeyed and got ready to
send Hagar away. He got up early
the next day and gave her some
bread and a bottle of water. He
told her and her son to go away.
So she went, but she did not know
where to go.

At last all the water in the
bottle was gone. Hagar could not
find any more water for her son to
drink. So she put him under a
bush and then went a good way
off and sat down. She was afraid
that her son was going to die. She
did not want to see him die. There

the poor mother cried.

But an angel of God called to her out of heaven and said to her, "What is the matter with you, Hagar? Do not be afraid. Get up."

Then God showed her where some water was. She went and filled the bottle with water and gave her son a drink. God helped the boy, and he grew.

Key:

angels — angel

make — making

Sound:

boy   boy's   bush   cried   die   drink

fun   grew   matter   must   named   sat

worked

Learn:

bottle   bread   gone   Hagar   Hagar's

off   ready

Lesson 10

A Hard Test

One day God told Abraham to
do a very hard thing. He said,
"Take your son, your only son
Isaac, the one whom you love, and
offer him for a burnt offering."
That meant he would need to kill
his son.

God told him to go to another
land and to take Isaac up on a
mountain. God would show him
which mountain it was to be.

This was a hard test for
Abraham. He loved Isaac very
dearly. But he loved God, too. God
gave this test to Abraham to see
whom Abraham loved the most.

Did he love God most, or did he love Isaac most? If he loved God more than Isaac, he would obey God. But if he loved his son better than God, he would not obey God by killing his only son. Do you know whom Abraham loved the most?

Key:

who — whom

Sound:

burnt   killing   offer   offering   test

Abraham Obeys

Even though Abraham loved Isaac very much, he loved God more. He was ready to do what God said he should do. He got up early in the morning and got ready to go.

Two men went with Abraham and his son Isaac. It took three days to get to the place where God wanted them to go. When Abraham could see the mountain, he told the two men to stay there where they were. He told them that he and Isaac would go and worship the Lord, and then they would come back to them again.

Then he and Isaac went on. On the way up the mountain, Abraham and Isaac talked to each other. Up on the mountain, Abraham made an altar. He put Isaac on the altar. Then he took the knife in his hand to kill Isaac.

Just as he was about to kill him, an angel called to him out of heaven and said, "Abraham, Abraham!"

Abraham answered, "Here I am."

The angel told him not to kill Isaac. How happy Abraham must have been! He looked around and saw an animal in a bush. It could not get out. Abraham took it and offered it to God instead of his son Isaac.

The angel talked to Abraham again. He told Abraham that because he had obeyed God, God would be with him. God was pleased with Abraham. He was pleased because Abraham obeyed Him even when He had asked him to do a very hard thing.

After this Abraham and Isaac went back to where they had left the two young men, and they went home together.

Key:

   obey — obeys

   worshiped — worship

Sound:

   knife   offered   pleased

Learn:

   altar   answered   young

A Man Sent

You remember that Abraham had left his home and father and brothers to come to the land of Canaan. But he must have thought of them many times and wondered how they were getting along.

One day he heard from someone that his brother and his wife had eight children. That was more than Abraham had, wasn't it? One of his brother's sons was already grown up and had a daughter whose name was Rebekah.

After Sarah was dead, Abraham wanted to help Isaac get a wife. He wanted Isaac to have a good wife. He wanted her to be from his people. So she must be from the land where his brother lived.

Abraham sent a man to get a wife for Isaac. The man was afraid he could not find a woman who would want to come back with him. But Abraham told him that God would help him.

Even though Sarah was already an old woman when God gave little baby Isaac to her, she lived a long time after Isaac was born. Isaac was about thirty-seven years old when his mother Sarah died.

Key:

all + *ready* = already

brother — brother's

daughters — daughter

bread — dead

who — whose

Sound:

eight   getting   grown   thirty-seven

times

Learn:

Rebekah   wasn't   woman   wondered

God Helps the Man

The man took ten camels and went. At last he came to the city where Abraham had lived. He took the camels to a well of water. It was the time of the day when women came to the well to get water.

The man did not know what woman God wanted for a wife for Isaac. So he prayed to God. He asked God to help him know which was the right woman. He told God that he would ask a woman for a drink. Then she would say, "Drink, and I will give your camels a drink, also." He asked God to let that be the woman whom He wanted to be a wife for Isaac.

While the man was still praying to God, a young woman came to the well. She had come to get some water. She went down to the well. She got some water and came back.

The man said to her, "Let me drink a little water."

The young woman answered, "Drink, and I will get water for your camels, too." So she got water for the camels, too.

The man asked her who she was. Can you guess who she was? She was Rebekah. Abraham's brother was her grandfather.

The man asked her whether there would be room for him to

stay at her house.

She told him that there was room and enough food for the camels to eat, too.

Now the man knew that God had helped him to find the right woman for Isaac. He bowed his head and thanked God.

Key:

Abraham — Abraham's

grand + *father* = grandfather

dead — head

Sound:

bowed   camels   guess   praying

thanked   whether

A Wife for Isaac

Rebekah ran home to tell her family what had happened at the well. Now they would get to hear more about her grandfather's brother who had left their land many years before.

When Rebekah's brother Laban heard Rebekah tell about the man at the well, he went to the well to find him.

Laban said to the man, "Come in. I have made room for you and your camels."

The man went with Laban. There they gave him something to eat. But he would not eat until he told them why he had come.

He told them that Abraham had sent him to this land to get a wife for his son Isaac. He told them how he had asked God to help him. He also told them how God had helped him.

Then Rebekah's father and brother knew that God wanted Rebekah to go with the man. So they said that she could go. They called Rebekah and asked her whether she would go with the man.

She said, "I will go."

The man took Rebekah, and they started back to the land of Canaan. Some other women also went along with Rebekah. When they got back home, the man told

Isaac what he had done. Isaac was glad to have Rebekah to be his wife. He took Rebekah to her new home. It was his mother's tent. Isaac loved his wife. God knew who would be a good wife for Isaac.

Abraham died about thirty-eight years after Sarah died. He was a godly man who had lived a long time.

Key:

grandfather — grandfather's

Rebekah — Rebekah's

Sound:

happened   Laban   thirty-eight

Twin Boys

For a long time Isaac and Rebekah had no children. They wanted children. Isaac asked the Lord for a child. The Lord was very good to them. He did not give them only one child. He gave them two children at the same time! They were twin boys.

Some twins look very much alike, but these twins were different. They looked different and they were different. Even their names were very different. One of them they named Esau, and the other one they named Jacob.

Esau grew up and was a very

good hunter. Isaac liked to eat the meat he would bring to him. Jacob was not a hunter like Esau. Rebekah loved Jacob very much.

Because of the way people did things at that time, Jacob and Esau would get Isaac's things when he died. But Esau would have a right to two times as much as Jacob. That meant Esau would get most of his father's things.

One day Jacob made some red soup. When Esau came in from the field, he was very tired. He was so tired that he thought he would die if he did not get something to eat. He saw the soup that his twin brother had made. He asked Jacob for some soup.

Now Jacob wanted the right to

have most of his father's things after Isaac died. So he said to Esau, "Sell me your right."

Esau thought it would be better to sell his right than to die. He sold the right to Jacob so that Jacob would let him have some of his soup. Then Jacob gave the soup to Esau, and Jacob had the right.

Key:

Isaac — Isaac's

Sound:

alike hunter meat names red sell
sold think tired twin twins

Learn:

Esau field Jacob soup

Isaac Moves

In the land where Isaac and
Rebekah and the twins lived, there
came a hard time. The people did
not have enough to eat. Before
Isaac was born, there had been a
time like this, too. At that time
Abraham and Sarah had gone
down to a strange land. There they
had food to eat.

But God did not want Isaac
and his family to go to this
strange land. God said, "Stay in
this land. I will be with you."
Isaac did not need to be afraid to
stay even if there was not much
food. God had promised to be with

him. God told him where to move so that he would have enough to eat. Isaac moved to a new place, but it was still in the land of Canaan. It was not in a strange land.

God kept His promise to Isaac. Isaac planted a crop. God made it grow and give them a lot of food. They had plenty to eat. Soon Isaac was a very rich man.

Key:

move — moves

stranger — strange

Sound:

crop   grow   planted

No Quarrels

The people in the land where Isaac lived saw that Isaac was rich. They didn't like it that he had more than they had. They wanted to be rich, too. That made them feel mean.

Isaac had some wells that had been his father's wells. These mean men filled up his wells with earth. Then Isaac couldn't get water from them.

At last the king of that land told Isaac to go away. So Isaac moved to a new place. It wasn't very far away. There he put up his tents.

Some of the men who worked for Isaac dug a well. It was a good well. Some other men came along, and they wanted that well. So they said, "This is our well."

Of course, the well didn't really belong to them. But Isaac wouldn't quarrel. He just had his men dig another well for him.

But the men took this well away from them, too. Still Isaac would not quarrel. He just moved to another place and dug another well.

After a time Isaac moved again. That night God came to Isaac and said, "I am the God of your father Abraham. Do not be afraid. I will be with you."

Key:

    could + *not* = couldn't

    did + *not* = didn't

    quarrel — quarrels

    would + *not* = wouldn't

Sound:

    dug   mean   wells

Learn:

    really

Rebekah's Plan

When Isaac was old, he could not see. One day he called Esau to him. Esau came to his father Isaac.

Isaac said, "I am old. I do not know when I will die. Go out to the field and get me some meat so that I can eat it. Then I will ask God to be with you and help you and give you good things."

Esau, the hunter, went out to the field to try to find some meat for his father.

Isaac's wife, Rebekah, heard what Isaac had said to Esau. But Rebekah loved her son Jacob. She wanted Isaac to ask God to give good things to Jacob instead of Esau. She thought of a plan. She would try to trick Isaac into praying for Jacob instead of Esau. Do you know what she did?

Sound:

trick

Rebekah Gets Jacob Ready

Rebekah said to Jacob, "I heard your father talk to Esau. He told him to bring him some meat so that he could ask God to do good things for him before he died. Now, my son, you do just what I tell you to do. Go and get two good young goats. I will make meat the way your father likes it. You take it to your father so that he can eat it and ask God to give you good things."

Isaac could not see. Rebekah thought he would think it was Esau when Jacob came in. But Jacob was afraid to do it. He was

69

afraid that his father would feel him and find out that he was not Esau. Then his father would know that he had told a lie. Then maybe his father would ask God to give him bad things and not good things. Jacob did not want that.

But his mother told him to obey her. So Jacob went out and got the kids. He brought them to his mother. She made the meat the way Isaac liked it. Then she took some of Esau's clothes and put them on Jacob. She did this so that if Isaac would feel him, he would think it was Esau. Then she gave the meat to Jacob to take to his father.

Key:

Esau — Esau's

get — gets

Sound:

kids   my

Learn:

clothes

Jacob Gets the Blessing

Jacob took the meat which his mother made ready and went to his father. He said, "My father."

His father said, "Here I am. Who are you?"

Jacob said, "I am Esau. I did what you told me to do. Please get up and eat of my meat so that you can bless me."

Isaac asked, "How did you find it so quickly, my son?"

"Because the Lord brought it to me," said Jacob.

"Come near so that I can feel whether you are really my son Esau or not," said his father.

Jacob went near and let his father feel him. Then Isaac said, "The voice is Jacob's voice, but the hands are the hands of Esau. Are you really Esau?"

Jacob said, "I am."

Isaac said, "Bring the meat near me so that I can eat it and bless you."

Jacob brought the meat to his father. His father ate it. Then he asked God to bless Jacob. That means he asked God to give him many good things.

Key:

Jacob — Jacob's

Sound:

ate   bless   blessing   hands   means

quickly   those   voice

Lesson 21

Esau Comes Home

As soon as Isaac had blessed Jacob, Esau came in from the field. He also had made meat the way his father liked it. He brought it to his father and said, "Let my father get up and eat of his son's meat so that you can bless me."

"Who are you?" asked Isaac.

"I am your son Esau," said Esau.

Poor old Isaac trembled very much. Then he said, "Who? Where is he who took meat and brought it to me? I ate before you came and blessed him. Yes, and he will be blessed."

When Esau heard this, he cried hard. He asked his father to bless him also.

But his father said, "Your brother came and took away your blessing."

Esau said, "He took away my right, and now he took away my blessing. Do you not have a blessing left for me?"

Isaac told Esau how he had blessed Jacob. He asked Esau what he should do for him.

Esau said, "Do you not have one blessing left for me, my father? Bless me, even me also, oh, my father!" And Esau cried again.

So Isaac gave him a small blessing. But it was very small.

Key:

come — comes

Sound:

blessed

Learn:

trembled

Jacob Leaves Home

Esau hated his twin brother Jacob. He hated him because he had taken the blessing away from him. Esau thought, "Soon my father will die. Then I will kill Jacob."

Rebekah found out that Esau wanted to kill Jacob. She called Jacob and said, "Your brother Esau plans to kill you. Now obey me and go to my brother Laban. Stay there until your brother is not angry any more. Then I will send and get you from there."

Isaac thought it would be best if Jacob would go to Laban. He thought it would be best if Jacob would get a wife there. He told Jacob to take one of Laban's daughters to be his wife. Then Isaac blessed Jacob again and sent him away.

Jacob went on his way to go to his uncle Laban. It was too far to get there in one day. After the sun went down Jacob stopped. He took some stones for pillows and lay down to sleep.

He dreamed he saw a ladder set up on the earth. The top of the ladder reached to heaven. Angels were on this ladder. Some were going up and some were coming down. God stood above it and talked to Jacob.

Key:

come — coming

hate — hated

Laban — Laban's

Sound:

dreamed found ladder lay leaves

pillows plans reached stones stood

Learn:

above uncle

God Talks to Jacob

The Lord said to Jacob, "I am the Lord God of Abraham your father and the God of Isaac. The land you are on I will give to you and to your children. I am with you and will keep you wherever you go. I will bring you back to this land."

After this, Jacob woke up. His dream made him afraid. He said, "The Lord is in this place, and I did not know it."

Jacob got up early. He took the stone that he had used for his pillow and set it up. He called the name of that place, Bethel.

Jacob wanted to go back home sometime without being afraid of Esau. He knew God would have to help him. Jacob made a promise to always worship God if God would help him. He said, "If God will be with me, and keep me in this way that I go, and give me food to eat and clothes to put on, so that I can come again to my father's house in peace, then the Lord shall be my God."

Then Jacob went on to the land where his uncle Laban lived.

Key:

  pillows — pillow

  talk — talks

  with + *out* = without

Sound:

  being   Bethel   dream   peace   stone

  woke

Learn:

  used

Jacob Meets Rachel

At last Jacob came to the land where Laban lived. He saw a well in the field. By the well were some sheep. People got water from this well for their sheep.

There was a big stone at the mouth of the well. Some men came and rolled back the stone. They gave the sheep water from the well. Then they put the big stone back on the mouth of the well.

Jacob talked to these men. He asked them from where they were. He asked them whether they knew Laban.

"We know him," they said.

"Is he well?" asked Jacob.

"He is well," they said. "And Rachel, his daughter, is coming with the sheep."

As Jacob was talking to these men, Rachel came with her father's sheep. She took care of them for her father.

Jacob went to the well and rolled back the stone from the mouth of the well. He gave Laban's sheep some water.

He talked to Rachel. He told her who he was. Rachel's father and Jacob's mother were brother and sister. Rachel ran to tell her father.

When Laban heard that his sister's son was at the well, he ran to meet him. He brought him to his house.

Key:

talk — talking

Sound:

meets   mouth   Rachel   Rachel's   rolled

sheep   sister   sister's

Lesson 25

A Mean Trick

Laban decided that Jacob
should have wages if he stayed
and worked for him. He asked
Jacob what his wages should be.

Laban had two daughters. The
older one was Leah. The other one
was Rachel. Jacob loved Rachel.
He wanted her to be his wife. So
he said, "I will work seven years
for Rachel."

Laban said, "It is better that I
give Rachel to you than to another
man. Stay with me."

Jacob worked seven years for
Rachel. But the seven years did
not seem long to Jacob because he

loved Rachel very much. After Jacob had worked seven years, he asked Laban to give him his wife.

But Laban tricked Jacob. He gave him a wife, but he did not give him Rachel. He gave him Leah.

Jacob did not like that. He had worked seven years for Rachel, and he wanted Rachel. He said to Laban, "What is this that you have done to me? Did I not work for Rachel?"

Laban said, "In our land we must not give the younger one before the older one. You may have Rachel, too, if you work for me seven more years."

Jacob worked seven more years for Rachel. He loved Rachel more than Leah.

Sound:

may   older   seven   tricked   wages

Learn:

Leah

Jacob Leaves Laban

Jacob had a big family. He had ten sons and one daughter.

For a long time Rachel did not have any children. This made Rachel sad. At last God gave her a baby boy. His name was Joseph. Then Jacob had eleven sons.

Jacob decided it was time for him to leave Laban. He wanted to go back to the land of Canaan where his father lived.

Jacob asked Laban to let him go. Laban did not want to let Jacob go. As long as Jacob was with Laban, God blessed Laban.

Jacob stayed and worked for

Laban.

But one day God said to Jacob, "Go back to the land of your fathers. I will be with you."

Jacob got ready to go. He put his wives and his children on camels. He took his animals and everything that he had. Rachel took her father's idols. Jacob did not know that she took them. Then they all left.

They did not tell Laban that they were going. He was away from home at the time, and he did not find out that they had left until the third day after they were gone.

Learn:

eleven   Joseph

Laban Goes After Jacob

On the third day after Jacob and his family left, Laban heard about it. He did not like it that Jacob had left and had not told him. But he had not been very nice to Jacob when he was there.

Laban and some other men went after Jacob. It took them seven days to get to him.

God talked to Laban in a dream. He told him to be careful how he talked to Jacob.

Laban asked Jacob why he had left and had not told him.

Jacob said, "I left because I was afraid you would take your daughters away from me."

"Why did you steal my idols?" asked Laban.

Jacob told Laban that he could look for anything that was his and take it. He also said that the one who had his idols should die. Jacob did not know that Rachel had them.

Laban went to look for his idols. He looked in Jacob's tent. He looked in Leah's tent. He looked in all the tents. He looked in Rachel's tent, too. He looked and looked but he did not find them. Where do you think they were? Rachel was sitting on them.

Key:

care + *full* = careful

Leah — Leah's

Sound:

goes   steal

Jacob Is Afraid

Jacob was angry with Laban. He did not like the way Laban had come after him. Jacob had worked hard for Laban, and Laban had not given him good wages for his hard work. If God would not have been so good to Jacob and helped him, Jacob would not have had very much.

But they promised that they would never hurt each other. They stayed in the mountain all night. Early in the morning Laban got up. He kissed and blessed his sons. Then he went home, and Jacob went on his way again. On the way the angels of God met him.

Jacob did not know whether Esau was still angry with him or not. He did not know whether he still wanted to kill him or not. He sent some men ahead to talk to Esau. He told them what they should tell him.

When the men came back, they said, "We came to your brother Esau. He is coming to meet you with four hundred men."

Now poor Jacob was very much afraid. He was afraid Esau and his men wanted to kill them.

Sound:
    ahead   hurt   kissed   met

Jacob and Esau Meet

Jacob was afraid of Esau. But he did what we should do when we are afraid. He prayed to God. He asked God to help them so that Esau would not kill them.

Then Jacob got a present ready to send to Esau. It was about five hundred eighty animals. There were different kinds of animals. This was a very big present. Jacob thought it would help Esau not to be angry with him any more. He sent some men on ahead with the present.

That night Jacob was all alone. Then a man came and wrestled with him. Jacob did not know who he was. They wrestled and wrestled until morning.

After they wrestled all night, the man put one of Jacob's hips out of joint. Then the man said, "From now on your name will be Israel." Then he blessed him and left. Now Jacob knew that it was God who had talked with him.

Jacob went on his way, and the sun came up. When he looked up, he saw his brother Esau. He had four hundred men with him. Jacob went to meet him. He bowed to the ground seven times. Esau ran to meet Jacob. He kissed Jacob, and they both cried. They seemed very happy to see each other. They talked together. Then Esau went back to his home. Jacob went on to the land of Canaan.

Key:

eight — eighty

Sound:

alone   ground   hips   joint   kinds
present

Learn:

both   Israel   wrestled

Lesson 30

Home at Last

After Jacob had been in
Canaan a little while, God told
him to go to Bethel. That was the
place Jacob had slept when he left
home because Esau wanted to kill
him. He had taken a stone for a
pillow. He had dreamed a strange
dream. God had talked to him.
Now God wanted him to go back
to Bethel to live there. God also
told him to make an altar.

Some people in his family had
idols. Jacob told them to get rid of
them. Then they would go to
Bethel. They gave their idols to
Jacob. Jacob took them and hid

them under a tree. Then they went to Bethel. Jacob obeyed God. He made an altar to God. God had said that he should.

After a time they left Bethel. As they were on the way, God gave Rachel another son. His name was Benjamin. Now Joseph had a baby brother, and Jacob had twelve sons.

But Rachel soon died. Now the wife that Jacob loved most was gone. They buried her near Bethlehem. Then they went on their way again.

At last Jacob came to his father Isaac. He had not seen him for twenty years.

When Isaac died, Jacob and Esau buried him.

Sound:

hid   rid   seen   slept   twelve

Learn:

Benjamin   Bethlehem   buried

Joseph and Jesus

Unit Five

Memory Verses

Lesson 1

Our Father which art in heaven, Hallowed be thy name.

Lesson 6

Thy kingdom come. Thy will be done in earth, as it is in heaven.

Lesson 11

Give us this day our daily bread.

Lesson 16

And forgive us our debts, as we forgive our debtors.

Lesson 21

And lead us not into temptation, but deliver us from evil.

Lesson 26

For thine is the kingdom, and the power, and the glory, for ever. Amen.

Matthew 6:9–13

Joseph's Dreams

Jacob loved Joseph very much. He loved him more than any of his other sons. He made him a coat of many colors.

Joseph's brothers knew that their father loved Joseph best. That made them hate Joseph. They could not even speak to him in a nice way.

Very often these brothers did things that were not right. Sometimes Joseph helped his brothers with the work. He saw the bad things they did. Then he told his father.

One time Joseph had a dream.

He dreamed they were binding sheaves in a field. His sheaf stood up. All the other brothers' sheaves stood around his sheaf. They bowed down to it. Joseph told his brothers what he had dreamed. It made them angry. They hated Joseph more than ever. They did not want Joseph to be a great man. They did not want to bow down to him.

Joseph dreamed again. He told his dream to his father and to his brothers. He said, "I have dreamed another dream. The sun, and the moon, and the eleven stars bowed down to me."

His father said, "What is this dream that you have dreamed? Shall I and your mother and brothers bow down to you?"

Joseph's brothers did not like it that Joseph had such wonderful dreams. But Joseph's father thought about this dream some more.

Key:

brother — brothers'

never — ever

Joseph — Joseph's

Sound:

binding dreams sheaf sheaves speak

Learn:

colors

Joseph Is Sold

Joseph's brothers were away from home taking care of their father's flocks. Jacob, whose name was now Israel, sent Joseph to them. He said, "See whether they and the flocks are all right."

Joseph went. When he got to the place where he thought they should be, he could not find them. A man saw Joseph looking for them. He asked, "For what are you looking?"

Joseph said, "I am looking for my brothers. Please tell me where they are."

The man told Joseph where to

look for them, and Joseph went. When Joseph was still a long way off, his brothers saw him. They said one to another, "Here comes this dreamer. Come now. Let us kill him. We will put him into a pit. Then we will say that some bad animal ate him. We shall see what will become of his dreams." You see, they thought that if they would kill him, his dreams would not come true, and they would not need to bow down to him.

But Joseph's oldest brother did not want to kill him. He said, "Let us not kill him. Let us just put him into a pit." When his brothers did not see him, he planned to take Joseph out of the pit so that he could go to his father again. But he did not tell his brothers this.

When Joseph came to his brothers, they took off his coat of many colors. Then they put him into a pit. There was no water in it.

As the brothers were sitting down to eat, they looked up and saw some people on camels coming. They were on their way to a strange land.

This gave one of the brothers an idea. He said, "What good will it do us if we kill our brother? Let us sell him."

The other brothers thought this was a good idea. They took Joseph up out of the pit and sold him to these strange men.

Poor Joseph felt very sad. He was going away with men he did not know. He was going farther and farther from home. And his own brothers had sold him.

Key:

be + *come* = become

take — taking

Sound:

dreamer   felt   flocks   oldest   pit

Learn:

idea   own

Joseph in Prison

The oldest brother, the one who wanted to let Joseph go back to his father, was not present when the other brothers sold Joseph. He did not know what they had done. When he came back to the pit, Joseph was gone. He felt very much afraid and sad about this.

The brothers took Joseph's coat. They killed a kid and dipped his coat in its blood. Then they took the coat to their father. They said, "We found this. Can you tell whether this is your son's coat or not?"

Yes, Israel knew that coat. He

said, "It is my son's coat. A bad animal has eaten him." For many days poor Israel cried. He did not know that his sons had not told him the truth. His children tried to make him feel better. But Israel felt very bad. He thought he would cry till he died.

But what had happened to Joseph? He was brought down to a strange land. There he was sold to one of the king's men. Now he was a servant. But God was with Joseph and helped him. His master could see this. He liked Joseph. God blessed him because Joseph was there with him.

Joseph's master made Joseph a great man. He let him do work that most servants would not get to do.

But Joseph's master had a bad wife. She tried to make Joseph sin. Day after day she tried. But Joseph did not want to sin. So he would not do what she said.

One day she tried very, very hard to make Joseph sin. But Joseph would not. God helped him.

Then this bad wife told the master a lie. She told him that Joseph had done a very bad thing. She did not tell him that she had tried to get him to do this bad sin, and he would not.

The master believed what his wife told him. He was angry with Joseph and had him put into prison. It was the prison where the king's prisoners were kept.

Key:

flood — blood

king — king's

Sound:

cry   dipped   eaten   its   kid   master

servant   servants   sin

Learn:

prison   prisoners

Two Dreams

God was with Joseph in prison. The keeper of the prison liked Joseph because God was with him and blessed all that he did. He told Joseph to look after the other prisoners.

One day the king in this strange land was angry with two of his men. He put them into prison. They were put into the same prison that Joseph was in. Joseph took care of them. One of these men had been the king's butler. The other man had been the king's baker.

In the same night, each of

these two men had a dream. But they did not know what their dreams meant. This made them sad.

In the morning, Joseph came in to where they were. He saw that they looked sad. He asked, "Why do you look so sad today?"

They said, "We each have dreamed a dream, and no one can tell us the meaning of our dreams."

Joseph told them that God could tell them what their dreams meant. So he asked them to tell him their dreams. The butler told his dream first. He said, "In my dream I saw a vine. In the vine were three branches. The vine had grapes on it. I took the grapes and pressed them into the king's cup. Then I gave the cup to the king."

Joseph said, "The three branches are three days. In three days you shall go back and work for the king. You shall give the cup to the king as you did before."

This was good news for the butler. He would not need to stay in prison very long any more. Joseph said to him, "Remember me when you are back in the king's house. Tell the king about me. I was stolen away from home. I have not done anything that I should be put into prison." Joseph thought that if the butler told this to the king, the king might let him out of prison.

The baker saw that the butler's dream meant something good. So he told his dream to Joseph. He said, "I had three white baskets on my head. In the top basket there were all kinds of baked things for the king. The birds ate them out of the basket on my head."

Joseph said, "The baskets are three days. In three days the king will hang you on a tree. The birds will eat you."

Sound:

baked   baker   basket   baskets

branches   butler   butler's   cup   grapes

hang   keeper   meaning   news   pressed

stolen   vine

The King Dreams

Everything happened just as Joseph said it would. In three days it was the king's birthday. He made a feast for all his servants. He let the butler be butler again. But he hanged the baker.

Do you remember what Joseph had asked the butler to do? He did not remember. He forgot Joseph.

Two years went by. Joseph was still in prison. Then the king had a dream.

He dreamed he stood by a river. He saw seven fat cows come up out of the river. They ate in a field. Seven other cows came up out of the river. But they were not fat as the first ones had been. They were very thin. The king had never seen such poor cows in all the land.

These thin cows did a strange thing. They ate up the seven fat cows. But they were still just as thin as they had been.

After this dream the king woke up. Then he went back to sleep. He dreamed again. In this dream he saw seven good ears of corn. They came up on one stalk. Then seven thin ears came up after them. The thin ears ate up the good ones.

The king woke up again and knew it was a dream. In the

morning, he was troubled. He wanted to know what these two dreams meant. He called in all his wise men. He told them his dreams. No one could tell him what they meant. Then the butler remembered something. What was it?

Key:

birth + *day* = birthday

years — ears

for + *got* = forgot

talk — stalk

Sound:

corn   cows   fat   feast

hanged   river   thin   wise

Learn:

troubled

Joseph Made Ruler

The butler remembered Joseph. He remembered that the baker and he had dreamed. Joseph had told them what their dreams meant. Everything had happened just as Joseph had said. The butler told the king about Joseph.

The king sent for Joseph. They hurried to get Joseph out of prison. Joseph cleaned up and put on other clothes. Then he came in to the king.

The king said to Joseph, "I have dreamed a dream and no one can tell me what it means. I heard that you can understand a dream to tell what it means."

Joseph said, "It is not in me. God shall give you an answer."

The king told his dreams to Joseph. He told about the seven thin cows that ate up the seven fat cows. He told about the seven thin ears of corn that ate up the seven good ears.

Joseph said, "The dream is one. God has showed you what He is about to do. The seven good cows and the seven good ears are seven years. The seven thin cows and the seven poor ears are seven years. In these seven years there will not be enough to eat.

"First, there will be seven very good years when there will be plenty to eat. After that will be

seven bad years. The people will not have enough to eat even with the seven years of plenty that they have just had."

Then Joseph told the king why he had dreamed two times. It was because the dream was from God. God would soon do this.

Joseph told the king he should look for a wise man to be a ruler over the land. The ruler should see that the people would have enough food. He should have men gather in lots of food in the seven good years. They should save it to eat when the seven bad years came.

Who do you think was the wise man whom the king set over this great work? Yes, it was Joseph. He made him ruler over all the land. Only the king was greater. The king gave Joseph a wife. Joseph and his wife had two sons.

Key:

rather — gather

great — greater

Sound:

cleaned   lots   over   ruler   save

Learn:

answer   hurried

Joseph Sees His Brothers

In the seven good years, Joseph gathered in very much food. They put the food into houses to keep it.

At last the seven good years were ended. Then came the seven poor years. They were not poor only in this strange land. They were poor in all the lands. Soon people did not have enough to eat. Then they came to Joseph for food. Joseph opened up the houses. He sold food to the people. Soon people came from other lands, too. They came to Joseph to buy food.

In the land of Canaan where

Joseph's father and brothers lived, they had poor crops, too. Israel heard there was plenty to eat in that strange land. He told his sons to go to that land and buy corn so that they would not die.

Joseph's ten brothers went to buy corn. Benjamin did not go along. Israel did not want him to go. He was the youngest. Israel was afraid something might happen to him. He had lost Joseph, and he did not want to lose Benjamin also.

Joseph was the ruler in the strange land. He sold corn to the people who came to buy. When Joseph's brothers came to buy corn, they came to Joseph. Because he was the ruler, they bowed down to him. Joseph knew who they were, but they did not know him. Joseph remembered his dreams. Now they were coming true. His brothers had bowed down to him.

Joseph did not know if his brothers were sorry they had sold him. He did not know if they would still hate him. So he tested them. He did not let them know who he was. He did not let them know that he knew who they were.

Key:

gather — gathered

house — houses

young — youngest

Sound:

crops   ended   happen   lost   tested

Learn:

buy   lose

Joseph Tests His Brothers

Joseph talked roughly to his brothers to test them. He asked them, "From where did you come?"

"From the land of Canaan to buy food," they said.

Joseph talked to them as if he thought they were telling him a lie.

But they said, "We all are one man's sons. We are true men. We came to buy food."

Joseph still talked to them as if he did not believe them.

"We are twelve brothers," they said. "We are the sons of one man in the land of Canaan. The youngest one is with his father. The other one is not living."

Joseph told them that he would test them. He said that he would see whether what they said was true. He told them they would need to bring their youngest brother down to him. Joseph kept them there three days. Then he said, "If you are true men, let one of your brothers stay here in prison. Then you go and take corn home. Bring your youngest brother to me, and you will not die."

The brothers talked together. They thought Joseph could not understand what they said because they had come from another land and did not speak the same as the people in this strange land. They felt very bad. They were having a hard time. They thought God was punishing them for the way they had treated Joseph. But Joseph did understand them and when he heard that, he went away and cried. Then he came back to them.

Joseph took one of the brothers and put him into prison. The other brothers saw him do it. He had to stay there until they brought Benjamin.

Joseph had some men fill his brother's sacks with corn. The brothers paid for the corn. Joseph had their money put back into their sacks, but the brothers did not know it.

Key:

have — having

punish — punishing

Sound:

fill   paid   sacks   tests   treated

Learn:

roughly

The Brothers in Trouble

At last the brothers started home. On the way home they wanted to feed their animals. One of the men opened his sack. He saw the money. "My money is given back to me," he said. The brothers were very much afraid. They said, "What is this that God has done to us?"

They went on to the land of Canaan. They told their father all the things that had happened to them. They told him about the brother who had to stay in prison until they took Benjamin along with them.

All the brothers took the corn out of their sacks. Then they all found their money in their sacks. It made them and their father very much afraid.

Poor Israel felt very sad. He thought Joseph was dead. And now they wanted to take Benjamin along with them the next time they went. He was afraid something might happen to Benjamin, too.

The oldest brother said, "Kill my two sons if I do not bring Benjamin back to you again."

But Israel, their father, said, "Benjamin shall not go down with you. His brother is dead. If anything should happen to him, you would bring down my gray hairs with sorrow to the grave."

Time went on. At last they had eaten all the corn. Their father said, "Go again. Buy us a little food."

One of the sons answered, "The man said that we can not see him unless our brother is with us. If you will send our brother with us, we will go. We will buy you food. If you will not send him, we will not go."

"Why did you tell him you had a brother?" asked their father.

They said, "The man asked us, 'Is your father yet alive? Do you have another brother?' So we told him. Could we know that he would say, 'Bring your brother down'?"

Then one of the brothers said

to their father, "Send the lad with us. We will get up and go so that we will live and not die. If I do not bring him back to you, I will always take the blame."

Poor Israel knew they needed the food. So he told them to go and take the man a present. He told them to take the money that was in their sacks besides more money to buy more corn. He told them to take Benjamin. He asked God to help them so that the brother in prison and Benjamin could come back home.

Key:

be + *sides* = besides

troubled — trouble

Sound:

blame   feed   grave   gray   hairs   lad

sack   unless

Learn:

sorrow

The Brothers Go Again

The brothers took the money, the present, and Benjamin and went down again into the strange land for food.

When Joseph saw that Benjamin was with them, he said to the ruler of his house, "Bring these men home and get ready. These men shall eat with me at noon."

The man did as he was told to do. He brought the men into Joseph's house. Joseph's brothers were afraid because they were brought into his house. They thought it might be because of the

money in their sacks. Maybe
Joseph thought they had stolen it.
Maybe he would punish them and
make them stay and be his
servants.

They came to one of Joseph's
helpers and said, "Oh, sir, we
came down the first time to buy
corn. When we opened our sacks,
we found money in them. We
brought it back again. We brought
other money to buy food. We can
not tell who put our money in our
sacks."

The man said, "Do not be
afraid. Your God and the God of
your fathers gave you money in
your sacks. I had your money."
Then he brought their brother who
was in prison out to them. He fed

their animals.

The brothers got their present ready to give to Joseph when they would eat with him at noon. When Joseph came home, they brought the present to him and bowed down to him.

Joseph asked, "Is your father well, the old man you talked about? Is he still alive?"

They answered, "Your servant, our father, is in good health. He is still alive." Then they bowed down to him again.

Joseph looked up. He saw his brother Benjamin. He asked, "Is this your younger brother of whom you told me?"

Then Joseph hurried and left the room because he had to cry.

He was so glad to see Benjamin
that he had to cry. But he did not
want anyone to see him cry. He
washed his face and went out to
them again.

Key:

wash — washed

Sound:

face   fed   noon   sir

Learn:

health

The Silver Cup

When the brothers sat down to eat, they were sitting in the order of their ages. The brothers could not understand how this could be. How did Joseph's helper know how old they were?

The food was brought to them. Benjamin was given five times as much food as the others. Everyone ate and had a good time with Joseph. But the brothers still did not know that this was Joseph.

Joseph said to his helper, "Fill the men's sacks with food. Give them all they can take. Put each man's money back in the top of his sack. Put my cup, the silver cup, in the top of Benjamin's sack."

Joseph's helper did just as he was told to do. The next morning, as soon as it was light, Joseph's brothers started home. Soon after they were gone, Joseph told his helper to go after them. He told him to ask them why they had taken his silver cup. He had been good to them.

The man went after them. He told them just what Joseph had said he should. He asked them why they had taken the silver cup.

The brothers said, "Why do you say that?" They had not stolen the cup, and they did not know that it had been put into Benjamin's sack. They said, "We brought back the money that was in our sacks. Then why would we steal silver or gold? Whoever has it, let him die, and we will be your servants."

But the man said, "Whoever has the cup will be my servant. The rest of you will not be blamed."

The brothers quickly took down their sacks. They opened them, and the man looked into the sacks. First he looked in the oldest brother's sack. It was not there. He looked in the next brother's sack. It was not there. Last of all he came to Benjamin's sack, and it was there. Yes, the cup was in

Benjamin's sack.

The poor brothers were very, very sad. What would their poor father say if they went back home and Benjamin was not with them? One of them had promised to bring Benjamin back. They were in great trouble. They all turned around and went back to talk to Joseph.

Key:

Benjamin — Benjamin's

every + *one* = everyone

who + *ever* = whoever

Sound:

blamed   gold   men's   order   silver

Learn:

ages

Joseph Tells Who He Is

The eleven brothers came back to Joseph's house. They fell down on the ground before him. Joseph asked, "What is this that you have done?"

Judah was the brother who had promised to bring Benjamin back home. He said to Joseph, "What shall we say? How shall we do? God has found out our sin. We are your servants, both we and the one who had the silver cup."

But Joseph said, "Only the man who had the silver cup will be my servant. The rest of you may go home to your father."

Joseph said this to test them. He wanted to see whether they loved Benjamin. They had not loved him before. Were they still so wicked?

Judah came near to Joseph. He told Joseph about their father. He told him how sad their father would feel if Benjamin did not come back with them. He said, "Benjamin's other brother is gone. His father feels sure he is dead. Now if Benjamin does not come home, I am afraid my father will die. I promised to bring Benjamin back home. Let me stay instead of Benjamin. I will be your servant. Let the lad go home with his brothers."

Then Joseph knew that his

brothers were not so wicked any more. So Joseph told all his helpers to go away from him. He wanted only his brothers to stay.

When Joseph was alone with his brothers, he started to cry. He cried so loudly that the people outside could hear him. Then he said to his brothers, "I am Joseph. Is my father still alive?"

His brothers could not answer because they were very much afraid.

Joseph did not want his brothers to be afraid of him. He loved them even if they had not been kind to him. He did not want to punish them.

Key:

out + *side* = outside

Sound:

feels   fell   loudly   wicked

Learn:

Judah   sure

Joseph Is Kind

Joseph was kind to his brothers. He told them to come near. They came near. He said, "I am Joseph your brother, whom you sold. Now do not be angry with yourselves for selling me. God sent me here so that you would not need to die.

"There have been two years of poor crops. There will be five more years of poor crops. God has sent me here so that you would have enough to eat. He made me ruler over this land. Now hurry and go back to my father. Tell him that God has made me ruler over this land. Tell him to come down to me."

He told all his brothers to come to this land to live. They were to bring their wives and children. He would take care of them and see that they had plenty to eat.

Joseph kissed Benjamin and cried. He kissed all his brothers and cried. After that his brothers talked to him.

Soon the king and his servants heard that these men were Joseph's brothers. They were pleased about it. They wanted all of them to come to their land to live. The king had Joseph give them wagons in which to move to this land. He gave them food and

clothes. Joseph sent a special present for his father. The brothers started back to the land of Canaan.

The sons came home to their father. What good news they had for him! They said, "Joseph is still alive. He is ruler over all the strange land." But Israel did not believe them. So they told him all the things Joseph had said. They showed him the wagons he had sent.

Then Israel believed them. He said, "It is enough. Joseph my son is still alive. I will go and see him before I die."

They started out. On the way they stopped to talk to God. That night God talked to Israel. He said, "Jacob, Jacob."

Jacob said, "Here I am."

God said, "I am God, the God of your father. Do not be afraid to go to the country where Joseph is. I will go with you and I will bring you back again."

They went on their way again. Jacob sent one of his sons on ahead to show them the way.

Joseph came out to meet his father. He was so glad to see his father that he cried a long time.

Jacob said, "Now let me die, because I have seen you, and you are still alive."

Key:

hurried — hurry

your + *selves* = yourselves

Sound:

selling   wagons

Learn:

country

Living and Dying
in a Strange Land

Joseph went to the king. He said, "My father and brothers and their flocks and all that they have are come." Joseph brought five of his brothers to the king.

"What is your work?" asked the king.

"We keep cattle," they said. "Both we and our fathers. We came here because we had no feed for our flocks. May we live in your land?"

Then the king said to Joseph, "Your father and brothers have come to you. Let your father and brothers live in the best part of the land."

Joseph brought his father to the king. Jacob blessed him.

Then the king asked Jacob, "How old are you?"

Jacob told the king he was one hundred thirty years old. Jacob did not think that was very old. His father, Isaac, had lived to be one hundred eighty years old. His grandfather, Abraham, had lived to be one hundred seventy-five years old.

Joseph let his father and brothers live in the best land. He saw to it that they had plenty to eat.

Jacob lived seventeen years in this strange country. Then the time

came near that he must die. He
called for Joseph. He told Joseph
not to bury him in this strange
land. He wanted to be buried in
the land of Canaan. That was
where his father, Isaac, had been
buried. That was where his
grandfather, Abraham, had been
buried. He wanted to be buried
beside them. Joseph promised to
do this.

Before Jacob died he blessed
all his twelve sons. He told them
what would happen to them in
their last days. Then he died. His
sons took him back to the land of
Canaan. There they buried him.

After this Joseph's brothers
were afraid again. They were afraid
that Joseph might hate them now

that their father was dead. Maybe he would try to pay them back for what they had done to him. Because they were afraid, they sent someone to talk to Joseph. They told him to tell Joseph that their father said he should forgive their sin. They told Joseph that they would be his servants.

But Joseph said, "Do not be afraid. You thought to hurt me, but God meant it for good. Because you sold me to this strange land, many people are saved alive. Do not be afraid. I will feed you and your little ones." Joseph talked very kindly to them.

After a while, Joseph knew he was going to die. He told his brothers that God would someday take them back to the land of Canaan. He told them to take his bones back to Canaan when they went. He wanted to be buried there.

Joseph died when he was one hundred ten years old.

Key:

be + *side* = beside

for + *give* = forgive

seven + *teen* = seventeen

Sound:

bones   cattle   kindly   saved

seventy-five

Learn:

bury   dying

Lesson 15

Jesus Is Born

For many, many years, people had been waiting for Jesus to come down from heaven to the earth. God had promised to send Him. At last it was time for Him to come.

He came as a little baby boy. He was born to a woman called Mary. God told Joseph, her husband, about it before Jesus was born. He told him to call His name Jesus because He would save His people from their sins. So, when the baby was born, they named Him Jesus.

Some wise men came to see

Jesus. They came from the East. They had seen His star and they wanted to worship Him. Jesus was born in a town called Bethlehem. The wise men did not know where to find Jesus. They went to Jerusalem which was not very far from Bethlehem. They asked at Jerusalem, "Where is He who is born King of the Jews? We have seen His star in the East and have come to worship Him." No one at Jerusalem seemed to know anything about Jesus.

There was a very wicked king at Jerusalem. He heard what the wise men had said. He called some Jews together. He asked them where Jesus would be born. They told him Jesus would be born in

Bethlehem.

The king called the wise men and told them to go to Bethlehem. He wanted them to look for Jesus until they found Him. He said, "When you have found Him, come and tell me so that I can come and worship Him, also."

After the king was through talking to them, they started out for Bethlehem. The star that they had seen in the East went before them and stopped just over the place where Jesus was. The wise men were very happy to see the star.

The wise men went into the house where Jesus was. They saw Jesus with His mother, Mary. They fell down and worshiped Jesus.

They had brought gifts for Him.
They opened them and gave Him
gold and other gifts.

Key:

news — Jews

Sound:

husband   sins   star   town   waiting

Learn:

Jerusalem   Mary   through

Jesus and the King

Do you remember what the king wanted the wise men to do after they found Jesus? God warned the wise men in a dream not to go back to the king. They did not go back to Jerusalem. They went back to their country another way.

This king was a wicked king. He did not really want to worship Jesus. He just pretended he did. He wanted to know where Jesus was so that he could kill Him. God knew that. That is why God told the wise men not to go back to the king.

After the wise men had gone, the angel of God came to Joseph in a dream. He said, "Arise, and take the young child and His mother and go to another country. Stay there until I tell you to come back. The king will look for the young child to kill Him."

Joseph got up in the night and took Jesus and Mary to another country. The king was very angry that the wise men did not come back to tell him where Jesus was. He wanted to be sure to kill Jesus, but he did not know where He was.

The king sent men to kill all the little boy babies in or around Bethlehem who were two years old or under. He thought Jesus was killed, too.

Many poor mothers cried because their dear little babies were killed.

When that wicked king was dead, an angel came to Joseph in a dream. He told him to go back to the land of Israel. The land of Israel is another name for the land of Canaan.

Joseph got up and took Jesus and His mother and went back to the land of Israel. When Joseph heard that the king's son was the new king, he was afraid. God warned Joseph in a dream not to go to the same place he had been. Joseph went up to Galilee to live. He lived there in a town called Nazareth.

Sound:

arise   pretended

Learn:

babies   Galilee   Nazareth   warned

John the Baptist

In those days John the Baptist came to preach. He told the people to be sorry for their sins. He told them not to sin any more.

John the Baptist's clothes were made of camel's hair. Such clothes would seem strange to us. His food would seem strange to us, too. He ate locusts and wild honey.

Many people went to hear this strange man. Many were sorry for their sins and told what they had done. Then John baptized them in the river.

John told the people about Jesus and that He would come.

Then Jesus went down from Galilee to the river where John was. He wanted John to baptize Him. John did not think he should baptize Jesus. He thought Jesus should baptize him. He had sinned, but Jesus had never sinned.

Because Jesus told John to baptize Him, John did. After Jesus was baptized, He went up out of the water. Then the Spirit of God came from heaven like a dove. It came down on Jesus. A voice from heaven said, "This is My Son, in whom I am well pleased."

After He was baptized, Jesus went out alone. He did not eat anything for forty days and forty nights. After that, He was hungry.

Satan came to Him and tried

to get Him to sin. Satan said, "If You are the Son of God, make these stones into bread."

But Jesus did not obey Satan. Jesus could make stones into bread, and bread would taste very good to a hungry person. But Jesus did not want to obey Satan. He wanted to obey His Father in heaven.

Jesus told Satan what the Bible said. Three times when Satan tried to get Jesus to sin, Jesus told him what the Bible said. Then Satan went away from Jesus, and angels came to help Him.

Key:

camel — camel's

money — honey

Sound:

baptize baptized hair locusts preach

sinned taste

Learn:

Baptist Baptist's hungry John

Jesus Preaches

One day Jesus heard that John the Baptist had been put into prison. Then Jesus went back to Galilee again. There Jesus began to preach. He told the people the same things John had said. He told them to be sorry for their sins. He told them to not do bad things any more.

When Jesus was by the Sea of Galilee, He saw two brothers. The name of the one brother was Peter. The name of the other one was Andrew. Peter and Andrew were fishermen. They were in a ship out in the sea where they tried to get fish in their nets.

Jesus said to them, "Come with Me and I will make you fishers of men." Jesus meant they should go to men and help them to know about God.

Right away they left their nets and followed Jesus. Soon He saw two other brothers. One was James and the other one was John. They were with their father in a ship fixing their nets. Jesus called to them. Right away they left the ship and their father and went with Jesus.

Jesus went all over Galilee. He preached to the people about God. He healed those people who were sick and came to Him. No matter what was wrong with them, Jesus could make them well.

Many people followed Jesus. They came from near and far. They liked to hear Jesus preach. Many of the things that Jesus said are in the Bible, and we can hear them, too.

Key:

names — James

Sound:

fishermen   fishers   fixing   healed   nets

Peter   preached   preaches   ship

Learn:

Andrew   followed

Jesus Heals People

One day a man who had leprosy came to Jesus. Leprosy was a bad disease. People who had leprosy did not get well. It got worse and worse until they died.

The man who had leprosy came to Jesus and worshiped Him. He said, "Lord, if You will, You can make me clean."

Jesus said, "I will; be clean." Right away the man's leprosy was gone.

When Jesus came to a town, another man came to him. This man was not sick, but he had a servant who was sick. The man told Jesus about his servant.

Jesus said to him, "I will come and heal him."

But this man did not feel he was good enough to have Jesus come into his house. He said to Jesus, "Just speak the word and my servant will be healed."

Jesus was pleased with what he said. He told the man, "Go your way; as you have believed it will be done to you." If the man believed that Jesus could make his servant well by just saying the word, that is the way it would be.

The man believed Jesus. And his servant was healed at the same time that Jesus said it.

When Jesus came to Peter's house, He saw Peter's wife's

mother lying down. She had a fever and was sick. Jesus touched her hand. The fever left her. She got up and was well.

Key:

Peter — Peter's

Sound:

clean   fever   heal   worse

Learn:

disease   leprosy   lying   touched

Everything Obeys Jesus

Jesus went into a ship. His disciples followed Him. A great storm came up on the sea. It was so bad that the ship was covered with the waves. The disciples were afraid. They thought that they might die.

Jesus had had a busy day. He was asleep. The disciples woke Him and said, "Lord, save us! We will die."

Jesus asked, "Why are you afraid?" He got up and told the wind and the sea to be quiet. Then everything was very still.

The disciples had never heard

of such a thing. They said, "What kind of Man is this that even the wind and the sea obey Him!"

When they came to the other side of the sea, two men met Jesus. They had devils living in them, and they lived where people had been buried. They were so bad that no one could come near them. When they saw Jesus, they called to Him.

The devils knew that Jesus might make them get out of the men. A long way off there were many pigs eating. The devils said to Jesus, "If You make us get out, let us go into the pigs."

Jesus said, "Go."

The devils came out of the men. They went into the pigs. The pigs ran down into the sea and died.

The men who took care of the pigs ran away and went into the city. They told the people what had happened to the men with the devils. They told what had happened to the pigs. Then the people of the city came out to meet Jesus. When they saw Him, they asked Him to go away.

Jesus went into the ship and went back to His own city.

Sound:

devils pigs side storm waves

Learn:

busy disciples

Jesus Doing Good

One time a ruler came to Jesus. He said, "My daughter is dead. But come, lay Your hand on her and she will live." Jesus and His disciples got up and went with this ruler. As they were going, a woman who had been sick twelve years came behind Him. She touched the hem of His clothes. She thought, "If I can just touch His clothes, I will be well."

Jesus turned around. When He saw the woman, He said, "Daughter, be of good comfort. Your faith has made you well." And the woman was well.

When Jesus came to the ruler's house, the people were making a lot of noise. They were crying because the ruler's daughter had died. Jesus did not want them to cry. He said, "The girl is not dead. She is sleeping."

Then the people laughed at Jesus and made fun of Him. But Jesus went in to where the girl lay. He took her by the hand, and she got up. Many people heard about this wonderful thing that Jesus did.

When Jesus went away from there, two blind men followed Him. They called to Jesus for help. When Jesus went into a house, they came to Him. Jesus asked them, "Do you believe that I am able to help you?"

They answered, "Yes, Lord."

Then Jesus touched their eyes
and said, "As you believe, it will
be done to you." Then their eyes
were opened, and they could see.
They went and told many people
about Jesus.

After this a man who had a
devil living in him was brought to
Jesus. The poor man could not
talk. Jesus made the devil go out
of the man, and then he could
talk. All the people thought about
the wonderful things Jesus was
doing. They could hardly believe it.
They said, "We never saw anything
like it!"

Many, many people came to
Jesus for help, and He healed

them. Jesus could heal every kind
of disease.

Key:

Jesus — Jesus'

ruler — ruler's

touched — touch

Sound:

able   comfort   crying   devil   faith   girl

hem   noise   sleeping

Learn:

eyes

The King and John the Baptist

Even the king heard about the wonderful things that Jesus did. The king in the land of Israel was a wicked man. He had a brother who had a wife. But the king took his brother's wife away from him because he wanted her to be his wife.

John the Baptist talked to the king about what he did. He said it was not right for the king to have his brother's wife.

The king did not like what John the Baptist said. His wife did not like John the Baptist. So the king put John in prison. He would have killed John, but he was afraid the people would not like it.

On the king's birthday, his wife's daughter danced for him. That pleased the king so much that he promised to give the girl whatever she would ask.

Her mother told her to ask for the head of John the Baptist. So the daughter said to the king, "Give me the head of John the Baptist."

The king was sorry. He knew that John was a godly man. But he had promised to give her whatever she asked, so the king had someone go to the prison and cut off John's head. Then it was brought to the girl, and she took it to her mother.

194

The disciples of John the Baptist came and got his body. They buried it.

Now when the king heard about Jesus and the wonderful things that He did, he thought it was John the Baptist. He said to his servants, "This is John the Baptist. He is risen from the dead. That is the reason he is doing so many wonderful works."

Key:

John — John's

Sound:

body   cut   danced   works

Learn:

reason

How Jesus Fed the Hungry People

When Jesus heard that John the Baptist was dead, He went away in a ship. He went to a mountain to be alone. But when the people heard where He was, they went to find Him. There were a great many people who came to Him. When Jesus saw them, He felt sorry for them and healed the ones who were sick.

In the evening His disciples came to Him and said, "This is a faraway place, and it is late. Send the people away so they can go to the towns and buy food."

But Jesus said, "They do not

need to go away. You give them something to eat."

They said to Jesus, "We have here only five loaves and two fishes." That would not be enough to feed very many people. There were about five thousand men there. And there were many women and children, too.

"Bring the loaves and the fishes to Me," said Jesus. They brought the food to Him.

Jesus told the people to sit down on the grass. He took the five loaves and the two fishes. Then He looked up to heaven and blessed the food. He broke the loaves and the fishes. He gave the pieces to His disciples, and they gave the food to the people. They kept giving more food until all the people had some. Everyone got enough to eat, and there was some left over.

When the people were finished eating, the disciples gathered up the food that was left. They gathered twelve baskets full. That was more food than they had before they began to eat.

After this, Jesus told the disciples to get into a ship and to start across the water. Then He sent the other people away.

Key:

far + $away$ = faraway

Sound:

across   broke   fishes   full   grass

late   loaves   sit   start   towns

Learn:

evening   pieces   thousand

Lesson 24

Walking on the Water

Jesus was alone in the mountain, and His disciples were in a ship in the middle of the sea. The disciples were having a hard time. The wind was making many waves, and the waves were tossing the ship.

Sometime that night Jesus went out on the water to the disciples. He did not go in a boat. He walked on the water. The disciples saw Jesus walking on the water, but they did not know who He was. Probably they had never seen anyone walking on the water. They thought they were seeing a spirit. This made them very much

afraid, and they cried out.

Right away Jesus said, "Cheer up. It is I. Do not be afraid."

Peter said, "Lord, if it is You, tell me to come to You on the water."

"Come," said Jesus.

Peter got out of the ship and started walking on the water to go to Jesus. He could walk on the water like Jesus. But then Peter took his eyes off Jesus. He saw how strong the wind was. He began to be afraid. Then he started to sink down into the water. Peter called to Jesus for help. "Lord, save me!" he cried.

Right away Jesus reached out His hand to Peter and caught him. Peter and Jesus both got into the ship. As soon as they were in the ship, the wind stopped.

Then the disciples worshiped Jesus. This helped them to be more sure that Jesus is the Son of God.

Sound:

caught   cheer   middle   seeing   sink

tossing   walked   walking

Jesus Talks to the Disciples

Do you remember what the king thought when he heard about Jesus? He thought that Jesus was John the Baptist.

One day Jesus asked His disciples a question. "Whom do men say that I am?" The disciples answered, "Some people say that You are John the Baptist. They think that You are risen from the dead. Some other people say that You are another prophet."

Then Jesus asked, "But whom do you say that I am?"

Peter knew who Jesus is. He said, "You are Christ. You are the

Son of the living God."

Jesus blessed Peter. He said
that it was God who showed Peter
what he knew.

Jesus took Peter and James and
John with Him to a high mountain.
Up there Jesus looked different.
His face began to shine like the
sun. His clothes were as white as
the light. Two men came and
talked to Jesus. But then a bright
cloud came and made a shadow
over them. A voice spoke from the
cloud. The voice said, "This is My
Son whom I love dearly, and in
whom I am well pleased. Listen to
Him."

When the disciples heard that,
they were very much afraid. They
fell down on their faces. But Jesus

came and touched them and said, "Get up. Do not be afraid."

When the disciples looked up, the other men were not there. Jesus was the only one they saw. They got up and went down the mountain with Jesus. As they were going down the mountain, Jesus told them not to tell anyone what they had seen. He wanted them to wait until later.

Jesus had told the disciples that He was going to be killed. He also told them that He would rise again in three days. Now Jesus told the disciples, "Do not tell anyone what you have seen on the mountain until I am risen again from the dead."

Sound:

faces   prophet   shadow

Learn:

listen

Some People Love Jesus

Jesus and His disciples were coming close to Jerusalem. Jesus sent two of the disciples into a town to find a colt for Him to ride. He told them, "You will find a colt tied as soon as you go into the town. Untie the colt and bring him to Me. If anyone says something to you, tell them, 'The Lord needs him.' Then he will let you have him."

The two disciples did as Jesus said. They went into the town and found a colt just as Jesus had said. They brought the colt to Jesus. The disciples put some

208

clothes on the back of the colt and Jesus sat on it. He rode on the colt to go into Jerusalem.

Very many people were going to Jerusalem. They loved Jesus. They wanted to praise Jesus. Some of them put clothes on the ground for Jesus to ride over. Some of them cut down branches from the trees and put them on the road. All the people that were going before Jesus and all the people that were coming after Him shouted. They praised Jesus like a king.

When they got to Jerusalem, everyone in the city heard about Jesus. They wondered about Him.

One day Jesus was at the house of a friend. While they were

eating a woman came to Him. She had some very precious ointment. She took the ointment and poured it on Jesus' head to show her love to Jesus.

The disciples did not like what she did. They thought she was wasting the precious ointment when she put it on Jesus' head. They thought it should have been sold to give the money to poor people.

Jesus was pleased with what the woman had done. He told the disciples that she had done a good work. Jesus said, "You always have the poor people with you, but you do not always have Me. This ointment she poured on Me is for when I will be buried." Jesus said that wherever God's Word is preached in all the world, they should tell what this woman did for Him.

Sound:

colt   ointment   ride   road   rode

shouted   tied   untie

Learn:

poured   precious   wasting

Some People Hate Jesus

Jesus had twelve disciples who were often with Him. One of them became a bad man. His name was Judas. He loved money more than he loved Jesus. He went to some of the men who hated Jesus. They wanted to kill Jesus. Judas asked them how much money they would give him if he would help them to kill Jesus. They promised to give him thirty pieces of silver. From that time on, Judas tried to find a chance to help them catch Jesus. Jesus knew what Judas was planning to do. He still loved him and treated him like a friend.

While Jesus and the disciples were eating together, Jesus told them that one of them would give Him away to the ones who hated Him. This made them very sad. They did not want to do such a thing to Jesus, their best Friend. They all asked, "Is it I?" When Judas asked Him, Jesus let him know that he was the one.

After supper, Jesus went with His disciples to a mountain. Jesus told them again that He was going to die. He also told them that He would rise again.

Jesus and His disciples came to a garden. He left most of them, while He and Peter and James and John went on farther. He told them that He was full of sorrow.

He told them to stay where they were and watch with Him. Then Jesus went a little farther and fell on His face and prayed. He said, "Oh, My Father, if it is possible, do not make Me go through this. Yet not what I want, but what You want, be done."

When Jesus came to the disciples, He found them sleeping. He said, "What? Could you not watch with Me one hour? Watch and pray."

Jesus went away and prayed two more times. Each time He came back to the disciples they were sleeping. The last time that He came back He told them that the time had come when He would be given to sinners.

While He was talking to them,
Judas came with many people.
They were coming to take Jesus
so they could kill Him. Judas had
told them that he would kiss the
One they wanted. So he went up
and kissed Jesus. Then the men
came and put their hands on Jesus
to take Him away.

Sound:

became   garden   kiss   planning
sinners   supper

Learn:

hour   Judas   possible   watch

What the Disciples Did

When Judas and the other men came to take Jesus away, one of the disciples wanted to help Jesus. He got his sword and was ready to fight. He reached out and hit the servant of the High Priest. He cut off the servant's ear. But Jesus did not want to fight. He told His disciple to put the sword away. Then Jesus touched the servant's ear and healed it.

The men took Jesus away. They led Him to the palace of the High Priest. The disciples were afraid and ran away. But Peter followed far behind. He went into the palace and sat with the servants to see what would happen to Jesus.

The Jews tried to find some reason to put Jesus to death. They tried to find someone to tell lies about Him. They found two men to lie about Him. The rulers and the people said He was bad and should die. They spit on Him. They hit Him. They made fun of Him. But Jesus did not get angry. He loved the people and felt sorry for them.

While Peter was sitting with the servants at the palace, a girl came to him and said, "You were with Jesus."

But Peter said, "I do not know what you are talking about."

After a time, another girl saw

him and said, "He was also with Jesus."

Peter said, "I do not know the Man."

Later another person came to Peter and told him that he was one of Jesus' disciples.

This time Peter said bad words, and he said that he did not know Jesus.

Right away the rooster crowed. Then Peter remembered something that Jesus had told him. Jesus had told Peter that he would say that he did not know Jesus. He would say it three times before the rooster crowed.

Peter felt sorry for what he had done. He went out and cried.

Judas knew that he had sinned

by giving Jesus to the men who wanted to kill Him. Judas wished he had not done it. He threw down the pieces of money and went and killed himself.

Key:

crow — crowed

ruler — rulers

servant — servant's

Sound:

himself   hit   lies   rooster   spit   threw

wished

Learn:

death   palace   priest   sword

Jesus Dies

In the morning, the Jews took Jesus to Pilate. They wanted him to let them kill Jesus. They told lies about Jesus. They tried to make it sound as though He were a bad man who should be killed.

But Pilate did not think Jesus was a bad man. He did not want to let them kill Jesus. He said he would let a prisoner go. The people could choose Jesus or another prisoner. The people said he should let the other prisoner go. Pilate asked, "Then what shall I do with Jesus?"

All the people shouted, "Kill

Him!"

Pilate asked, "Why? What has He done that is bad?"

The people shouted again, "Kill Him!" So Pilate let the Jews have their way. Pilate told the soldiers to kill Jesus.

They spit on Jesus, hit Him, and made fun of Him. They gave Him bitter vinegar, but He would not drink it. They took Him out and nailed Him to a cross to die. Then they sat down to watch Him. They had a sign up over Jesus' head that said, "THIS IS JESUS THE KING OF THE JEWS." Two bad men were killed with Jesus. One was on a cross on the right side of Jesus. The other one was on a cross on the left side of

Jesus.

At noon it became very dark. It stayed dark for three hours. Then Jesus died. When he died, the earth shook and people were afraid.

In the evening, a rich man came to Pilate and asked for Jesus' body. He was Jesus' friend, and he wanted to bury Him. He wrapped the body in a clean cloth and put it in a new grave. He put a big stone in front of the grave. Then he went away.

Key:

hour — hours

Sound:

bitter cloth cross dies front nailed
shook sign sound wrapped

Learn:

Pilate soldiers vinegar

Jesus Is Alive

The next day some Jews came to Pilate. They said that they remembered that Jesus had said He would rise again in three days. They were afraid Jesus' disciples would steal His body away at night. Then they would tell people that Jesus rose again. The Jews wanted Pilate to make sure that could not happen. They asked him to have someone watch the grave for three days, so no one could steal Jesus' body.

Pilate said, "You may have someone to watch. Go, and make it as sure as you can."

So they went and sealed the stone at the grave. They had some men stay there all the time to make sure that no one came to steal the body.

Very early on Sunday morning many things happened. An angel came down from heaven. He rolled away the big stone from the front of the grave. Then he sat upon the stone. The face of the angel was very bright, and his clothes were as white as snow.

The men who had stayed to watch the grave were so afraid they shook and became like dead men.

That morning, some of the women who loved Jesus came to the grave. The angel told them not to be afraid. He said, "I know that you are looking for Jesus. He is not here. He is risen as He said. Come and see where He lay. Go quickly and tell His disciples that He is risen and you can see Him in Galilee."

The women quickly went away to tell the disciples. How happy they were! Their best Friend was alive again. On the way they met Jesus. Jesus talked to them, and they worshiped Him.

The disciples went to Galilee. There they saw Jesus, and Jesus told them what to do. He wants all His friends to tell the other people about Him. He wants them to teach others to do all the things He told them to do.

Key:

$sun + day =$ Sunday

Sound:

rose   sealed   snow   teach

Word Lists

The Letters *K, S,* and *L* before each word stand for the following words respectively: *Key, Sound, Learn.* The new words are listed under these headings after each lesson in the reader, and their meanings are explained in the introduction to units 4 and 5 in the teacher's manual.

Unit 4

1

L	Abram	*S*	seemed	*L*	wherever
L	Abram's	*S*	started	*L*	worshiped
L	before				
K	brother		**2**		**3**
L	Canaan	*L*	believed	*S*	along
S	died	*K*	belong	*K*	another
L	different	*L*	enough	*S*	better
S	got	*S*	far	*L*	decided
S	hard	*L*	instead	*S*	Lot's
S	leave	*S*	king	*L*	money
S	left	*S*	later	*L*	move
S	Lot	*S*	plain	*L*	moved
K	maybe	*K*	remembered	*S*	needed
S	part	*L*	stranger	*S*	prayed
K	promised	*L*	strangers	*L*	quarrel

L quarreled
S room
S tent
S tents
L their
L together
S while

4

K anyone
S choose
S chooses
L city
K fight
S look
S looked
S pay
S plenty
L rather
S seem
S such
K taken
S than
S well

5

L Abraham
K believe

S born
K hundred
L Isaac
L meant
L nearly
S new
S pass
L Sarah
K year

6

K anything
S behind
S child
S hot
S knows
L laugh
L laughed
S loud
S meet
S ran
S saw
L shall
S sitting
K someone
S tree
L visit
L wash

7

L course
S fifty
S five
S forty-five
S less
L once
S prays
S ten
S thirty
L thought
S twenty

8

L angels
S around
S brought
S burned
L daughters
L early
S fire
S hand
S salt
S smoke
S sons-in-law
S stayed
S tried
S turned

9

K angel
L bottle
S boy
S boy's
L bread
S bush
S cried
S die
S drink
S fun
L gone
S grew
L Hagar
L Hagar's
K making
S matter
S must
S named
L off
L ready
S sat
S worked

10

S burnt
S killing
S offer

S offering
S test
K whom

11

L altar
L answered
S knife
K obeys
S offered
S pleased
K worship
L young

12

K already
K brother's
K daughter
K dead
S eight
S getting
S grown
L Rebekah
S thirty-seven
S times
L wasn't
K whose
L woman

L wondered

13

K Abraham's
S bowed
S camels
K grandfather
S guess
K head
S praying
S thanked
S whether

14

K grandfather's
S happened
S Laban
K Rebekah's
S thirty-eight

15

S alike
L Esau
L field
S hunter
K Isaac's
L Jacob
S meat

S names
S red
S sell
S sold
L soup
S think
S tired
S twin
S twins

16

S crop
S grow
K moves
S planted
K strange

17

K couldn't
K didn't
S dug
S mean
K quarrels
L really
S wells
K wouldn't

18

S trick

19

L clothes
K Esau's
K gets
S kids
S my

20

S ate
S bless
S blessing
S hands
K Jacob's
S means
S quickly
S those
S voice

21

S blessed
K comes
L trembled

22

L above
K coming
S dreamed
S found
K hated
K Laban's
S ladder
S lay
S leaves
S pillows
S plans
S reached
S stones
S stood
L uncle

23

S being
S Bethel
S dream
S peace
K pillow
S stone
K talks
L used
K without
S woke

24

S meets
S mouth
S Rachel
S Rachel's
S rolled
S sheep
S sister
S sister's
K talking

25

L Leah
S may
S older
S seven
S tricked
S wages

26

L eleven
L Joseph

27

K careful
S goes
K Leah's
S steal

28

S ahead
S hurt
S kissed
S met

29

S alone

L both
K eighty
S ground
S hips
L Israel
S joint
S kinds
S present
L wrestled

30

L Benjamin
L Bethlehem
L buried
S hid
S rid
S seen
S slept
S twelve

Unit 5

1

S binding
K brothers'
L colors
S dreams
K ever
K Joseph's
S sheaf
S sheaves
S speak

2

K become
S dreamer
S felt
S flocks
L idea
S oldest
L own
S pit
K taking

3

K blood
S cry
S dipped

S eaten
S its
S kid
K king's
S master
L prison
L prisoners
S servant
S servants
S sin

4

S baked
S baker
S basket
S baskets
S branches
S butler
S butler's
S cup
S grapes
S hang
S keeper
S meaning
S news

S pressed
S stolen
S vine

5

K birthday
S corn
S cows
K ears
S fat
S feast
K forgot
S hanged
S river
K stalk
S thin
L troubled
S wise

6

L answer
S cleaned
K gather
K greater
L hurried

233

S lots
S over
S ruler
S save

7

L buy
S crops
S ended
K gathered
S happen
K houses
L lose
S lost
S tested
K youngest

8

S fill
K having
S paid
K punishing
L roughly
S sacks
S tests
S treated

9

K besides
S blame
S feed
S grave
S gray
S hairs
S lad
S sack
L sorrow
K trouble
S unless

10

S face
S fed
L health
S noon
S sir
K washed

11

L ages
K Benjamin's
S blamed
K everyone
S gold
S men's

S order
S silver
K whoever

12

S feels
S fell
L Judah
S loudly
K outside
L sure
S wicked

13

L country
K hurry
S selling
S wagons
K yourselves

14

K beside
S bones
L bury
S cattle
L dying
K forgive
S kindly

S saved
K seventeen
S seventy-five

15

S husband
L Jerusalem
K Jews
L Mary
S sins
S star
L through
S town
S waiting

16

S arise
L babies
L Galilee
L Nazareth
S pretended
L warned

17

L Baptist
L Baptist's
S baptize
S baptized

K camel's
S hair
K honey
L hungry
L John
S locusts
S preach
S sinned
S taste

18

L Andrew
S fishermen
S fishers
S fixing
L followed
S healed
K James
S nets
S Peter
S preached
S preaches
S ship

19

S clean
L disease
S fever

S heal
L leprosy
L lying
K Peter's
L touched
S worse

20

L busy
S devils
L disciples
S pigs
S side
S storm
S waves

21

S able
S comfort
S crying
S devil
L eyes
S faith
S girl
S hem
K Jesus'
S noise
K ruler's

S sleeping
K touch

22
S body
S cut
S danced
K John's
L reason
S works

23
S across
S broke
L evening
K faraway
S fishes
S full
S grass
S late
S loaves
L pieces
S sit
S start
L thousand
S towns

24
S caught
S cheer
S middle
S seeing
S sink
S tossing
S walked
S walking

25
S faces
L listen
S prophet
S shadow

26
S colt
S ointment
L poured
L precious
S ride
S road
S rode
S shouted
S tied
S untie
L wasting

27
S became
S garden
L hour
L Judas
S kiss
S planning
L possible
S sinners
S supper
L watch

28
K crowed
L death
S himself
S hit
S lies
L palace
L priest
S rooster
K rulers
K servant's
S spit
L sword
S threw
S wished

29

S bitter
S cloth
S cross
S dies
S front
K hours
S nailed

L Pilate
S shook
S sign
L soldiers
S sound
L vinegar
S wrapped

30

S rose
S sealed
S snow
K Sunday
S teach

Alphabetical Order

Unit 4

a

above
Abraham
Abraham's
Abram
Abram's
ahead
alike
alone
along
already
altar
angel
angels
another
answered
anyone
anything
around
ate

b

before
behind
being
believe
believed
belong
Benjamin
Bethel
Bethlehem
better
bless
blessed
blessing
born
both
bottle
bowed
boy
boy's
bread
brother

brother's
brought
buried
burned
burnt
bush

c

camels
Canaan
careful
child
choose
chooses
city
clothes
comes
coming
couldn't
course
cried

crop

d
daughter
daughters
dead
decided
didn't
die
died
different
dream
dreamed
drink
dug

e
early
eight
eighty
eleven
enough
Esau
Esau's

f
far
field

fifty
fight
fire
five
forty-five
found
fun

g
gets
getting
goes
gone
got
grandfather
grandfather's
grew
ground
grow
grown
guess

h
Hagar
Hagar's
hand
hands
happened

hard
hated
head
hid
hips
hot
hundred
hunter
hurt

i
instead
Isaac
Isaac's
Israel

j
Jacob
Jacob's
joint
Joseph

k
kids
killing
kinds
king
kissed

knife
knows

l

Laban
Laban's
ladder
later
laugh
laughed
lay
Leah
Leah's
leave
leaves
left
less
look
looked
Lot
Lot's
loud

m

making
matter
may
maybe

mean
means
meant
meat
meet
meets
met
money
mouth
move
moved
moves
must
my

n

named
names
nearly
needed
new

o

obeys
off
offer
offered
offering

older
once

p

part
pass
pay
peace
pillow
pillows
plain
plans
planted
pleased
plenty
prayed
praying
prays
present
promised

q

quarrel
quarreled
quarrels
quickly

r

Rachel
Rachel's
ran
rather
reached
ready
really
Rebekah
Rebekah's
red
remembered
rid
rolled
room

s

salt
Sarah
sat
saw
seem
seemed
seen
sell
seven
shall
sheep

sister
sister's
sitting
slept
smoke
sold
someone
sons-in-law
soup
started
stayed
steal
stone
stones
stood
strange
stranger
strangers
such

t

taken
talking
talks
ten
tent
tents
test

than
thanked
their
think
thirty
thirty-eight
thirty-seven
those
thought
times
tired
together
tree
trembled
trick
tricked
tried
turned
twelve
twenty
twin
twins

u

uncle
used

v

visit
voice

w

wages
wash
wasn't
well
wells

wherever
whether
while
whom
whose
without
woke
woman
wondered

worked
worship
worshiped
wouldn't
wrestled

y

year
young

Unit 5

a
able
across
ages
Andrew
answer
arise

b
babies
baked
baker
Baptist
Baptist's
baptize
baptized
basket
baskets
became
become
Benjamin's
beside
besides
binding
birthday

bitter
blame
blamed
blood
body
bones
branches
broke
brothers'
bury
busy
butler
butler's
buy

c
camel's
cattle
caught
cheer
clean
cleaned
cloth
colors
colt

comfort
corn
country
cows
crops
cross
crowed
cry
crying
cup
cut

d
danced
death
devil
devils
dies
dipped
disciples
disease
dreamer
dreams
dying

e

ears
eaten
ended
evening
ever
everyone
eyes

f

face
faces
faith
faraway
fat
feast
fed
feed
feels
fell
felt
fever
fill
fishermen
fishers
fishes
fixing
flocks

followed
forgive
forgot
front
full

g

Galilee
garden
gather
gathered
girl
gold
grapes
grass
grave
gray
greater

h

hair
hairs
hang
hanged
happen
having
heal
healed

health
hem
himself
hit
honey
hour
hours
houses
hungry
hurried
hurry
husband

i

idea
its

j

James
Jerusalem
Jesus'
Jews
John
John's
Joseph's
Judah
Judas

244

k

keeper
kid
kindly
king's
kiss

l

lad
late
leprosy
lies
listen
loaves
locusts
lose
lost
lots
loudly
lying

m

Mary
master
meaning
men's
middle

n

nailed
Nazareth
nets
news
noise
noon

o

ointment
oldest
order
outside
over
own

p

paid
palace
Peter
Peter's
pieces
pigs
Pilate
pit
planning
possible
poured

preach
preached
preaches
precious
pressed
pretended
priest
prison
prisoners
prophet
punishing

r

reason
ride
river
road
rode
rooster
rose
roughly
ruler
rulers
ruler's

s

sack
sacks

save

saved

sealed

seeing

selling

servant

servants

servant's

seventeen

seventy-five

shadow

sheaf

sheaves

ship

shook

shouted

side

sign

silver

sin

sink

sinned

sinners

sins

sir

sit

sleeping

snow

soldiers

sorrow

sound

speak

spit

stalk

star

start

stolen

storm

Sunday

supper

sure

sword

t

taking

taste

teach

tested

tests

thin

thousand

threw

through

tied

tossing

touch

touched

town

towns

treated

trouble

troubled

U

unless

untie

V

vine

vinegar

W

wagons

waiting

walked

walking

warned

washed

wasting

watch

waves

whoever

wicked

wise

246

wished	worse	**y**
works	wrapped	youngest
		yourselves